Monkeys and Apes

Words by Dean Morris

Raintree Childrens Books
Milwaukee • Toronto • Melbourne • London

Library of Congress Number: 77-8148

8 9 10 11 12   88 87 86 85

Printed and bound in the United States of America.

Library of Congress Cataloging Publication Data

Morris, Dean.
  Monkeys and apes.

  (Read about)
  Includes index.
  SUMMARY: An introduction to various species of
monkeys and apes and their behavior in the wild.
  1. Monkeys—Juvenile literature. 2. Apes—
Juvenile literature. [1. Monkeys. 2. Apes.] I. Title.
QL737.P9M62   599'.82   77-8148
ISBN 0-8393-0005-0 lib. bdg.
ISBN 0-8393-0286-X softcover

This book has been reviewed
for accuracy by

Dr. Merlin D. Tuttle
Curator of Mammals
The Milwaukee Public Museum

John M. Condit
Curator, Division of Reptiles and Amphibians
Museum of Zoology
The Ohio State University

Monkeys and Apes

tarsier

Monkeys and apes may look different from each other in some ways, but they are all related.

All of them belong to a group of animals called primates.

People are primates too.

baboon

Some primates are
very smart animals.
They are able to find many
ways to get food and
make homes for themselves.
In these pictures you can
see that monkeys and apes
are alike in some ways.

gorilla

woolly monkey

These animals are called prosimians. They are like some of the earliest primates that lived before there were monkeys and apes. They usually live in trees and look for food at night.

The tree shrew looks a little like a squirrel.

tree shrew

bush baby

The bush baby has big eyes and ears. It can protect its ears by folding them up. The bush baby jumps from branch to branch. On the ground, it hops like a kangaroo.

The slow loris lives in forests in warm parts of the world. It moves about slowly at night. In the daytime the loris curls itself into a ball and sleeps.

loris

potto

The potto is another slow-moving animal. Like the loris, the potto has strong thumbs and toes. It uses them to hold onto branches. The potto can hang upside down for a long time.

indri

Lemurs are prosimians that live in Madagascar, an island east of Africa, and the Comoro Islands.

One group of lemurs, called indri, lives in forests. Sometimes several indris live together in a pack.

Indris have large hands and feet. They look as if they are wearing gloves. They have no tails. When they come down from the trees, they walk on their long hind legs.

Ring-tailed lemurs live on the ground in rocky places. Like the indris, ring-tailed lemurs sometimes live in groups. They take care of each other and keep each other clean.

When a ring-tailed lemur senses danger, it gives off a strong smell. The smell warns the other ring-tailed lemurs.

ring-tailed lemurs

owl monkey

Monkeys belong to two groups, New World and Old World.

Most New World monkeys have flat noses and long tails. They usually live in Central or South America. The owl monkey is a New World monkey. It is the only monkey that is active at night.

golden lion marmoset

Marmosets are known for their loud, high voices.

The golden lion marmoset is about the size of a cat. It has a silky mane. Its fur is golden.

The squirrel monkey has a small body and a long tail. The tail helps the monkey balance itself. At night, the monkey wraps its tail around itself.

squirrel monkey

hairy saki

The hairy saki has long, thick hair. It grows over the saki's shoulders like a cape. Its tail is bushy.

When the hairy saki is asleep, it looks like a pile of dead leaves.

The uakari lives in the jungles along the Amazon River. Little is known about this animal. There are three kinds of uakaris. One kind has red fur and a bright red face. Another kind has brown fur and a black face. The third kind has gray fur and a pink face. They have no fur on their faces. They all have short tails. They live in small groups and usually stay in the high branches of trees.

uakari

spider monkey

Spider monkeys are the best climbers of the New World monkeys. A spider monkey's tail is like another arm. Spider monkeys can pick things up with their tails. They use their tails to hold onto branches. They can swing from tree to tree. Sometimes they hold tails, just as we hold hands.

Spider monkeys sleep close together. They sleep with their tails around their necks.

Howler monkeys are very noisy. The males have enlarged bones in their throats. The bones help them make a booming noise. Howlers also roar and bark.

Howler monkeys live high in the trees. They often march in lines along the branches. They don't often come down from the trees. When a howler wants a drink, it hangs by its tail over a stream or pond.

howler monkeys

Most Old World monkeys are found in Africa and Southeast Asia.

One kind of Old World monkey is the macaque. Barbary apes are macaques. They live in North Africa and on the Rock of Gibraltar.

Some macaques live near rivers or beside the sea.

Barbary apes

long-tailed macaque

Most macaques like water. They swim well. They dive for crabs and seaweed to eat. Macaques also eat plants and insects.

Some macaques live in the forest or jungle. Most have long tails. They hold onto branches and swing through the trees.

When people cut down the forests, macaques may go into nearby towns to find food. They take food from garbage piles.

Some Old World monkeys are leaf-eaters. Monkeys that are leaf-eaters have large stomachs. They must eat a lot of leaves to get enough food.

The colobus monkey is a leaf-eater. So is the langur. Some langurs can go a long time without drinking. They get their water from the leaves they eat.

colobus monkeys

langur

Another leaf-eater is the proboscis monkey. Male proboscis monkeys have noses that hang down below their chins. At times they have to push their noses out of the way to eat. Proboscis monkeys like swimming. They lie in the sun after a swim.

proboscis monkey

Mangabeys live in the forests of Africa. Some of them are plain gray. Others are black and have bright clumps of hair. All mangabeys have white eyelids.

Mangabeys eat fruit. They have pouches in their cheeks. They store food in the pouches.

mangabeys

Guenons are small jungle monkeys. They are found in Africa. Some guenons have bright-colored hair. Some have mustaches or beards.

Guenons live in large groups during the day. They separate at night.

Guenons eat plants and fruit. Like the mangabeys, they have pouches in their cheeks.

guenons

a baboon
family group

Baboons live in groups too. One or several big males are the leaders. The others obey them. Baboons are large monkeys that like the ground better than the trees. They eat stems and leaves. They also dig underground for roots to eat. They are very good at finding water.

Mandrills also live in family groups. They are very fierce monkeys. Groups of mandrills have been known to kill leopards and other large animals.

Both mandrills and baboons live in Africa.

mandrill

The apes are the largest primates. Apes have small tails or no tails at all. They use their toes and fingers almost like people do.

Gibbons are apes. They live in the rain forests of Asia. They have thick coats that keep out the rain. Gibbons are the best acrobats in the forest. Their long arms are very strong. Gibbons can travel fast, swinging from branch to branch.

gibbon

Gibbons also move along on their hind legs. They run on very thin branches high in the trees. They look like tightrope walkers in a circus.

gibbon

Gibbons can jump long distances. They look as if they are flying. Some gibbons can leap as far as 30 feet (about 9 meters).

Gibbons live in small families. Each family has its own part of the forest. Gibbons hoot to keep other animals away.

There are several different kinds of gibbons. The largest gibbon is called the siamang. The siamang lives in the highest parts of trees. It has a pouch in its throat. It can blow the pouch up like a balloon. This helps the siamang to hoot louder.

siamang gibbons

orangutan

The orangutan lives in the swampy forests of Sumatra and Borneo. It is the largest animal that spends most of its time in trees. In fact, the orangutan doesn't often leave the trees. It is very clumsy on the ground.

The orangutan is very heavy, but its arms are strong. It can swing through the trees.

Every night the orangutan makes a new nest for itself in a tree.

Orangutans build nests even when they live in zoos.

Scientists want to put more orangutans in zoos. That is because orangutans are disappearing. People hunt them. Too many have been killed. The orangutans that are still alive need to be protected.

chimpanzee

Chimpanzees are smaller than orangutans. They live in Africa. They climb trees to get food. They sleep in trees too. But, unlike orangutans, chimps often walk on the ground.

In the wild, chimps live in large family groups. The chimps clean each other. Older chimpanzees take care of the young.

Chimps can "talk" to each other by making sounds. They say things by making faces too.

Many chimpanzees are kept in zoos. They are playful and fun to watch. Chimpanzees are very intelligent apes. People have been able to teach them to do many things.

Gorillas are the largest of the apes. Some grow as tall as people. Gorillas are stronger than people. They have long arms and powerful chests.

Gorillas live in families. The strongest gorilla is the family leader. When they are left alone, gorillas are shy and quiet. They live in two areas of Africa.

gorillas

Like orangutans, gorillas may die out. We must protect the gorillas and other monkeys and apes. Otherwise these animals will disappear from the earth.

The Life Span
for Some Monkeys and Apes in Captivity

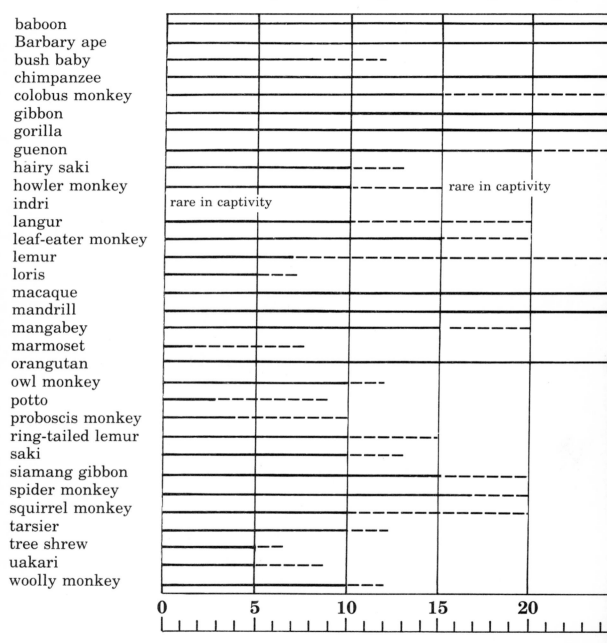

baboon
Barbary ape
bush baby
chimpanzee
colobus monkey
gibbon
gorilla
guenon
hairy saki
howler monkey
indri
langur
leaf-eater monkey
lemur
loris
macaque
mandrill
mangabey
marmoset
orangutan
owl monkey
potto
proboscis monkey
ring-tailed lemur
saki
siamang gibbon
spider monkey
squirrel monkey
tarsier
tree shrew
uakari
woolly monkey

rare in captivity

rare in captivity

0   5   10   15   20

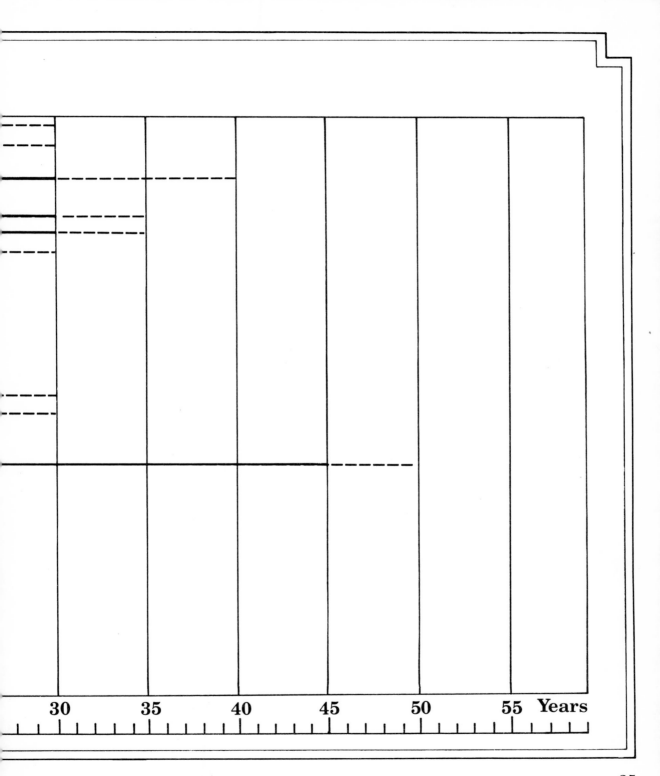

30   35   40   45   50   55   **Years**

Where to Read About the Monkeys and Apes

baboon (ba bo͞on′) *pp. 4, 22, 23*
Barbary ape (bär′ bə rē   āp) *p. 16*
bush baby (boosh   bā′ bē) *p. 6*
chimpanzee (chim′ pan zē   *or*   chim pan′ zē)
   pp. 30-31
colobus monkey (ko′ lə bəs   mung′ kē) *p. 18*
gibbon (gib′ ən) *pp. 24-27*
golden lion marmoset (gōld′ ən   lī′ ən
   mär′ mə set′) *p. 11*
gorilla (gə ril′ ə) *pp. 5, 32-33*
guenon (gə nōn′) *p. 21*
hairy saki (her′ ē   sa′ kē) *p. 12*
howler monkey (hou′ lər   mung′ kē) *p. 15*
indri (in′ drē) *p. 8*
langur (läng gyoor′) *p. 19*
leaf-eater monkey (lēf′ ēt′ ər   mung′ kē)
   pp. 18, 19
lemur (lē′ mər) *pp. 8-9*
long-tailed macaque (lông tāld   mə kak′   *or*
   mə käk′) *p. 17*

loris (lōr′ əs *or* lôr′ əs) *p. 7*

macaque (mə kak′ *or* mə käk′) *pp. 16-17*

mandrill (man′ drəl) *p. 23*

mangabey (mang′ gə bā *or* mang′ gə bē) *p. 20*

marmoset (mär′ mə set′) *p. 11*

New World monkey (noo wurld mung′ kē)
pp. 10-15

Old World monkey (ōld wurld mung′ kē) *pp. 10,
16-23*

orangutan (ô rang′ oo tan′) *pp. 28-29*

owl monkey (oul mung′ kē) *p. 10*

potto (pot′ ō) *p. 7*

proboscis monkey (prə bos′ əs mung′ kē) *p. 19*

ring-tailed lemur (ring′ tāld′ lē′ mər) *p. 9*

saki (sa′ kē) *p. 12*

siamang gibbon (sē′ ə mang′ *or* sē am′ əng
gib′ ən) *p. 27*

spider monkey (spī dər mung′ kē) *p. 14*

squirrel monkey (skwur′ əl mung′ kē) *p. 11*

tarsier (tär′ sē ā′ *or* tär′ sē ər) *p. 4*

tree shrew (trē shroo) *p. 6*

uakari (wä kä′ rē) *p. 13*

woolly monkey (wool′ ē mung′ kē) *p. 5*

Pronunciation Key for Glossary

a	a as in **cat**, **bad**
ā	a as in **able**, ai as in **train**, ay as in **play**
ä	a as in **father**, **car**
e	e as in **bend**, **yet**
ē	e as in **me**, ee as in **feel**, ea as in **beat**, ie as in **piece**, y as in **heavy**
i	i as in **in**, **pig**
ī	i as in **ice**, **time**, ie as in **tie**, y as in **my**
o	o as in **top**
ō	o as in **old**, oa as in **goat**, ow as in **slow**, oe as in **toe**
ô	o as in **cloth**, au as in **caught**, aw as in **paw**, a as in **all**
oo	oo as in **good**, u as in **put**
o͞o	oo as in **tool**, ue as in **blue**
oi	oi as in **oil**, oy as in **toy**
ou	ou as in **out**, ow as in **plow**
u	u as in **up**, **gun**, o as in **other**
ur	ur as in **fur**, er as in **person**, ir as in **bird**, or as in **work**
⟂o͞o	u as in **use**, ew as in **few**
ə	a as in **again**, e as in **broken**, i as in **pencil**, o as in **attention**, u as in **surprise**
ch	ch as in **such**
ng	ng as in **sing**
sh	sh as in **shell**, **wish**
th	th as in **three**, **bath**
t͟h	th as in **that**, **together**

GLOSSARY

These words are defined the way they are used in this book.

acrobat (ak′ rə bat′) a person who does stunts
  that take strength and skill
active (ak′ tiv) moving about; full of action
alike (ə līk′) the same as; in the same way
alive (ə līve′) living; not dead; having life
ape (āp) a large, tailless Old World monkey
area (er′ ē ə) a certain place or part of
  something
balance (bal′ əns) to keep a steady position
beard (bērd) hair that grows on the chin
  and cheeks
body (bod′ ē) the whole of a person, animal,
  or plant
bone (bōn) a hard, stiff part of the skeleton of
  most animals with backbones
booming (boom′ ing) a deep, hollow sound
bushy (boosh′ ē) thick; spreading out like a bush
cheek (chēk) the part of a person's or animal's
  face below the eye

chest (chest) the front, upper part of a
person's or animal's body

chimp (chimp) a short word for chimpanzee, a
small ape that lives in trees

chin (chin) the part of a person's or animal's
face below the mouth and above the neck

climber (klīm′ ər) a person or animal able to
move upward to the topmost part of something

clump (klump) several things in a group
or bunch

clumsy (klum′ zē) not graceful; awkward

crab (krab) a hard-shelled water animal
with five pairs of legs, the first with
a pair of claws

dead (ded) without life; no longer living

dive (dīv) to go down through water headfirst

doesn't (duz′ ənt) does not

enlarge (en lärj′) make or become bigger

eyelid (ī′ lid′) a fold of skin that can cover
or uncover the eye

family (fam′ ə lē *or* fam′ lē) people or
animals all related to each other who may live
together as a group

garbage (gär′ bij) food and other things that are thrown away

glove (gluv) a hand covering with separate parts for fingers and thumb

gray (grā) the color that is made when black and white are mixed together

hind (hīnd) at the back; rear

hoot (hōōt) to make a sound like an owl's call

insect (in′ sekt) a small animal with a hard outer covering and without a backbone, such as a fly or ant, and usually with six legs and two or four wings

intelligence (in tel′ ə jəns) knowing, understanding, and being able to think clearly

itself (it self′) that same one

jungle (jung′ gəl) land in warm, damp places covered with many trees, vines, and bushes

kangaroo (kang′ gə rōō′) an animal with small front legs, strong back legs used for leaping, and a long tail used for balance

known (nōn) understood as a fact

leaf (lēf) one of the flat, green parts that grow from a plant stem *plural* **leaves**

leaves (lēvz) more than one leaf; see **leaf**

leopard (lep′ ərd) a large cat that has a
 brownish-yellow coat with black spots

male (māl) of the sex that can father young

meter (mē′ tər) a measure of length equal to
 about 39 inches

monkey (mung′ kē) a member of the primate
 group, not including man and also usually
 not including lemurs and tarsiers

mustache (mus′ tash *or* məs tash′) hair
 that grows between the mouth and nose

obey (ō bā′) to do what someone says
 must be done

onto (ôn′ to͞o *or* on′ to͞o) to a place on
 top or above

otherwise (uth′ ər wīz′) if not; or else

plain (plān) common; ordinary; not colorful

playful (plā′ fəl) full of play

pouch (pouch) a hollow, baglike part in
 the bodies of some animals

powerful (pou′ ər fəl) full of power;
 very strong

primate (prī′ māt) an animal belonging to

the most advanced scientific classification
of mammals

prosimian (prō sim′ ē ən) an animal belonging
to the less advanced group of primates

related (ri lā′ tid) belonging to the same
group of living things

root (ro͞ot *or* root) the part of a plant
that grows underground

seaweed (sē′ wēd′) a plant that grows
in salt water

sense (sens) when a person or animal knows
about the changes in its surroundings
through hearing, seeing, smelling, tasting,
or touching

separate (sep′ ə rāt′) to keep apart; to divide

shy (shī) easily scared

silky (sil′ kē) looking or feeling like silk;
smooth

stem (stem) the main part of a plant that
holds up the leaves and flowers

stomach (stum′ ək) the part of a person's
or animal's body where food goes after it
is swallowed

stream (strēm) water that flows along in
a course

swampy (swom′ pē) soft and wet; like
a swamp

themselves (t̲hem selvz′ *or* t̲həm selvz′) the
same ones

throat (thrōt) a small space behind the mouth
through which air and food passes

thumb (thum) a finger that is shorter and
thicker than the other fingers on some
animals' hands, used along with other fingers
to grasp, hold, and pick up things

tightrope (tīt′ rōp′) a tightly stretched rope
or wire placed above the ground

travel (trav′ əl) to move from one place to
another

underground (un′ dər ground′) a place below
the surface of the earth

upside down (up′ sīd′ doun′) turned so the
top part of something is on the bottom

warn (wôrn) to tell ahead of time that
something might happen

wild (wīld) wilderness; parts of the earth where living things grow naturally without the help of people

wrap (rap) to put a covering all around something

Bibliography

Alston, Eugenia. *Growing up Chimpanzee.*
New York: Thomas Y. Crowell Company, 1975.

Borea, Phyllis. *Seymour, a Gibbon: About
Apes and Other Animals and How You Can Help
to Keep Them Alive.* New York: Atheneum
Publishers, 1973.
Using a gibbon in the New York City ASPCA
as an example, it describes the characteristics
of primates in general and gibbons specifically
and discusses the organization and function
of the ASPCA and the need for wildlife conservation.

Burton, Maurice, and Burton, Robert, editors.
The International Wildlife Encyclopedia.
20 vols. Milwaukee: Purnell Reference Books, 1970.

Conklin, Gladys. *Little Apes.* New York:
Holiday House, 1970.

D'Aulaire, Emily, and D'Aulaire, Ola.
Chimps and Baboons. Edited by Russell
Bourne and Natalie S. Rifkin. Washington,
D. C.: National Wildlife Federation, 1974.

Robinson, Nancy K. *Jungle Laboratory: The
Story of Ray Carpenter and the Howling Monkeys.*
New York: Hastings House Publishers, 1973.
Describes the observations made by scientist
Ray Carpenter on the behavior of howler
monkeys in their natural habitat.

Schick, Alice. *Siamang Gibbons: An Ape Family.*
Milwaukee: Westwind Press, 1976.
Traces a family of gibbons from the Sumatran
jungle to the Milwaukee County Zoo.

Shuttlesworth, Dorothy. *The Story of Monkeys, Great Apes, and Small Apes*. Garden City, N.Y.: Doubleday & Company, 1972.
Discusses the distinguishing physical characteristics, habits, and environments of various species of monkeys and apes.

Thompson, Brenda. *Monkeys, Gorillas, and Chimpanzees*. Minneapolis: Lerner Publications Company, 1976.

Wilson, Jean. *Animals of Warmer Lands*. Reading, Mass.: Addison-Wesley Publishing Company, 1969.